MY TWO SISTERS

MY TWO SISTERS

THEIR ENERGY STILL FLOWS

AUTHOR AND BROTHER

MICHAEL C RICHARDS

To Patricia, Lee and Rhian
Without your love and patience this book
would never have been written.

My two sisters, one day we will be together.

www.michaelcrichards.com

ISBN 9781913532345

Cover design by Ben Hargreaves
Typeset by seagulls.net
Project management by whitefox

An early Celtic image of twins with their spirits entwined

The Celtic Knot

These knots were found on the architecture and book illumination of the Byzantine Empire in the East, which was founded in 350AD.

Further examples of the Celtic Knots can be found in Ethiopian art, Russian book illumination in the Medieval era and also in Islamic art.

There is a strong theory among historians that the pre-Christian Celts drew these particular symbols because they were not allowed to create other images, indeed some scholars say the early Celtic religion was similar to Islam in that realistic depictions of living creatures were forbidden.

The Celtic knotwork pattern is said to represent the interconnection of life and our place within the Universe.

The Celtic spiral represents an individual's accomplishment to balance his inner and outer self and it also reflects on his/her personal spirit or spirits aligned to that individual, **their twin.**

For me there is a personal interest in the Celtic knot. A good few years ago, when I dug my old school books out of the loft, I noticed that on my little Collins dictionary I had scrawled a few random sketches, that I now realise were my early attempts at the Celtic knot. They appeared on my maths homework book and bizarrely a front and back cover, no pages, of Jane Austin's pride and prejudice. The Celtic knot was on the inside of the cover on both pages.

My artistic skills appeared to develop with age and I found that I had concentrated on one particular design of knot. That is shown above.

Was this an early recognition of my twin sister's presence?

To my dear friends and family, thank you

I have written this book to unashamedly try to understand what has happened in my sixty-four years of life. The story starts on the day I was born, the day my twin sister died.

I was aware of something from an early age, but I never realised until now how much she has helped me through these sixty-four years on this mortal coil. That was my fault, the sixty-four years have gone in a blink and survival has been my main goal. Life has been hard: sometimes I was so close to giving up on the opportunity that I was given. My twin sister saved me more than once, from my illogical thoughts and their possible disastrous consequences. I didn't acknowledge her presence right up until 2015. I was too busy, a stupid statement in itself but please take a moment to look at your own lives, time goes so quickly, and make sure you enjoy your time on this planet.

My recognition of my sister happened when my life came close to its final moments in Mallorca in 2015. I suppose it was appropriate that it was in Porto Cristo, the Port of Christ.

This part of my life has already been well documented in my book, *Hallucinations or Reality* and so I do not need to dwell on it here. The fact that I found out about the presence of my older sister after its publication was an enormous shock to my system.

I have so much information to commit to paper that I envisage the project will take me at least three years. I will try to publish a book on all the developments each year. That is the aim driving me forward; at sixty-four years of age I am still in the learning stage of life. I find it hard to believe, is it enjoyable? Some days yes, some days no, and on some occasions the information destroys my will to live, but it is my passion that helps me overcome the negativity.

The one thing I have found to my benefit since the incident in Mallorca is that I understand a lot more about my life and the presence of my sisters. I believe I have made inroads on understanding my older sister's hatred of me, but most of all I want to survive long enough to explore all the information I have been given, both by my research team and by so many friends.

I hope this explains why I feel I am in a rush and cannot tolerate delays: if something comes up that needs my attention, I do it immediately.

This one line of text affects us all:

'Life is too Short.'

Don't waste it.

Acknowledgements

Firstly, my immediate family, who are always there when I need them. Without their support this book would never have been written.

My family in Cardiff and Cornwall, your help has been fantastic. It might just be small points that you mention from time to time, almost hardly worth telling me, but they open up huge areas that just needed that slight turn of the key.

My friends who have put up with my boring conversations and obsession with my two sisters, I probably won't stop boring you...

Finally, to my mum and dad: this book is not written with malice – you supported me in everything I did. You may have shown it in strange ways, but let's not forget you did all you could to help me develop.

I love you both.

Life is great; life can be a bitch...
Do we manage life or does it manage us?

I have tried, on the following pages, to explain in a brief synopsis what has happened on the journey of events since I found out about my older sister's possible presence in the world.

It has been a frightening but informative journey. The world in which we live, and think we understand, this world we can cope with. Yet there is the possibility of another world, parallel with ours, that we really know nothing about.

Two eminent scientists, Ervin Laszlo and Anthony Peake, have researched and studied the existence of this parallel world. I would highly recommend their book, *The Immortal Mind*. It is the study of science and the continuity of consciousness beyond the brain. They describe things far better than I can and use words that identify areas I really struggle to explain. Technically, it is a far better description of life after death.

One thing I have identified is that the psychic industry or 'mediums' as they may be called is very secretive. However, at the same time there is a commercialised sector of the life and death industry. I won't dwell on the commercialised side; it is full of false hope that generates income for the purveyors of this false information.

The psychic and hypnotherapist I worked with were extremely worried about their security, and rightly so. Would you invite a total stranger into your house to talk about these things? While remaining cool and comfortable, I couldn't, and I'm not sure I would even want to. The income they recoup, to my mind, is danger money. I don't think they charge enough for genuine results. They are examining your brain when all is said and done.

Everything I have written in this book is true, as accurate as I can make it, and, in all honesty, what I can remember. It does come as a shock to your system. Trying to adapt to the information is where the trick lies.

Names of most of the people involved in the psychic industry have been changed, all by their own request and in some cases, their insistence. Again, security is essential for them.

Please bear in mind that the main publication of the book will go into far more detail than I have here. This book is simply to satisfy people's initial thoughts about what I have discovered. The information trail is very much alive and I shall carry on writing in my diary all the relevant events that take place, either under my instigation or because of the research team finding a key and opening another door.

My father and mother

It has been extremely hard to write about my parents. We all love our parents, I hope. Mine raised me, and I think they did a very good job. I hope my children can say the same about myself and my wife, Pat.

My father and mother had problems, the main one being they didn't have any money. This was through no fault of their own. They certainly tried to make ends meet. I can't really say how many jobs my mother had when I was young – there seemed to be so many. The same with my father: he worked in a warehouse, a shop, and on some dog racing tracks. That bit I didn't understand and have never followed up. The dog racing world was a mystery to me and still is.

We lived in a little downstairs flat and had one small coal fire. We took it in turns to change in front of the fire when alone in the room to hide all our modesties. Well, I assume that was why. I recall the great excitement when we got a gas fire. It meant immediate heat, and, for me, no more collecting sticks and logs then waiting for my dad to come home and get the fire lit. I quickly learnt how to synchronise turning the knob and pressing the ignition, though I did get told off quite often for having it on when my mum and dad came home from work.

Life was simple, but good, or so I thought. When I was seven years old my mother suffered a 'trauma' and I didn't see her for four months, she was locked in her bedroom. A nervous breakdown was the main rumour, but no one was allowed to see her, which included me as well as the rest of the family. The doctor only attended once from what I remember.

The thing I realise now but not at the time, or I suppose I didn't realise the seriousness of it, was that my dad was having an affair. I knew the woman, she played a big part in my life. I didn't realise that they were so close. My mother did, but I must stress I don't think my mum's trauma and my dad's affair coincided.

I had no real clue at the time, life was all football on the green outside, things may have been going on but I didn't have a care in the world.

I cannot offer any excuses for my dad: life was indeed hard, a constant struggle. I would say as a couple they did well to survive life's trials and tribulations. That will to survive has certainly rubbed off on me, and for that I am grateful.

Were we a normal family? I think so, it didn't occur to me that we were different. Maybe other people felt different but they all had the same goal in our close-knit street: recovery from the War and survival by any means you could.

I loved my dad and mum then and I still do now. I hope to meet them later on in a possible new life. There are many questions I would like to ask.

'MY TWO SISTERS'

AUTHOR MICHAEL C RICHARDS

THEIR BROTHER

There are very few moments in anyone's life that can compare.

To communicate with your twin sister who died at birth, sixty-four years on, is quite momentous. To then find out when you have published your first book in 2016 that you had an older sister by five years, this is enough to blow any human being's mind. I am that human being and I am still trying to come to terms with this incredible information.

Where do you start to relate this story, so that it makes sense to people? Maybe even give comfort to many, I hope.

Please bear with me, I am going to outline what I have found out through my research team, my family, public records, a psychic, a hypnotherapist and so many other people along the way. Their help in particular has restored my faith in mankind, people helping people, another small miracle in these manic times in which we live

In my first book, which came about because I had entered the inner sanctum of death, I recognised the presence of my twin sister. It was of no use to me or anyone close to me, I was more or less declared insane and would lead a vegetable existence.

Through this current text I hope to dismiss some of the questions that were raised in my first book and pointed to my insanity. The vegetable existence was overcome by today's medical science.

There will be further books to follow. My twin sister will ensure that there are further publications. She has a lot to say and it has to be channelled through me. I am her eyes, her ears, her body, but her mind and emotions remain part of her.

My twin sister is a positive energy source, but my older sister is a negative presence. I have had no communication with her. I do not know at this point if she is alive or dead. My twin sister tells me she is an energy source very much like her, which would suggest she is dead. By the end of this book I may have evidence to assist me in that decision. I passionately hope so.

This is very much the start of a journey. I do not believe it is possible to put a timescale on the completion of the journey, with so much new information being recorded daily.

The journey will take us back to the Second World War. It will encompass my birth alongside my twin sister and it will travel through my life until the present day.

Some people may lose interest on the way, so I intend to make this book purely factual. No ramblings, just facts. I will elaborate on situations more precisely in the planned trilogy of books. This, I hope, will appease the current trend in the world: the information needs to be there now, no delay, and if it's not on page one of Google, it is history it seems.

If you are looking for a quick and easy answer to the big question, 'Is there life after death?' I would respectfully ask you to put this book down, forget about it and return at a later date, as the remaining books are published. I don't have a definitive answer. I will be relaying my experiences but it's up to you to draw your own conclusion.

The present time – 2019, my sixty-fourth so far on this mortal coil

My sister made contact with me on the banks of the Hennerton backwater, it was very pleasant.

It was September. Early in the morning, I was walking back from my VegPod area – the squirrels had done more damage to my corn on their stalks, which was pretty frustrating. The sun was shining and I sat on the banks of the backwater. It was peaceful, not a sound. A mother swan brought her new babies up to see me, seven of them. She looked proud, as any mother would, the father hung around at the back, just keeping a watchful eye.

I know it's stupid to write this but I did talk to the mother swan – she obviously didn't answer. Mary, my twin sister, was with me, her warm glow emanated within and around me, a slight little dig in the ribs, not a physical dig but more of an energy surge against my stomach wall, reminding me that I was being stupid talking to animals. As I walked away, I felt the energy that she had created invigorate my body. It's hard to explain, but it is like no other pick-you-up that mass corporations try to cram into a bottle.

I had felt a similar feeling back in early July. We had gone strawberry picking: my wife Pat, my son Lee, myself and the five grandkids. It was fun, again the sun was shining. The kids were running in all directions, shouting and laughing at each other. They were all so busy finding their strawberries they didn't notice me walk away. I walked to the end of the field and just watched them, not a care in the world, it was a wonderful moment. Mary's presence was strong, the warm glow was present, my mind was clear, she communicated her thought. It was short and to the point: 'Michael, don't leave me, I need you.' The tear in my eye would have been clearly visible to anyone passing but I was happy, very happy. I walked back to the kids all shouting at me, 'Gramps, look at this one. Gramps, look at how many I've got...' Bliss.

I felt calm, relaxed and, the main thing, normal. My sister was with us, the family together.

Mary's presence in my life – 2019

This does need explaining and is not straightforward. I feel I am not clever enough to do justice to the description of Mary's presence but I will relay my thoughts. I feel her energy – it is like warm water washing around inside you. She can use that energy to hold you, to energise you, to display her feelings. She cannot talk, so she communicates by thought. It has been frustrating trying to communicate this way. I feel she has lost her temper with me on occasions, because my head was cluttered with too many thoughts and I was asking and replying to her questions before she had finished what she wanted to communicate. We have managed, and by trial and error learnt to communicate slowly for a limited time span since we both get tired quite quickly with the transfer of thoughts.

I have had two prolonged discussions with her since our first, which was under the guidance of the psychic. She can display her emotions to me in various ways, these emotions ranging from sadness, joy, anger, but most of all humour.

I have asked her a question which had been bothering me. Is she inside me? Does she control my thoughts? Her reply was given to me in a straightforward way: 'No, you are the life form, I live off you, and my body is the energy around you. You control my thoughts. I learn from you. Without you, Michael, I don't know what will happen, that scares me.' That has stuck with me. It does answer some questions but there are so many more I need to ask her. I need a clear mind, which is far easier said than done. I think she was saying, 'I need more of your attention, I need more time with you.' A very simple view but maybe not too far off. I don't know at this moment, but I hope to find out as our relationship develops.

Emotional guilt – August 2019

I have detailed the pleasant, nice times. The next two are short and sharp. I have had to cope with how they changed in such a short amount of time.

When my wife Pat and I arrived in Mallorca, I wanted to speak to Mary and feel her presence. The ideal situation was on the very edge of Cala Egos, where the vast Mediterranean Sea laps into a small bay. I have never seen anyone there whenever I have been, so it was ideal isolation. I sat on the rocks and could see so far I cannot even gauge the distance. A rock pool started splashing in front of me. It was Mary showing off. I believe it is her energy flow that does this. Then I felt her glow envelop my body – we were together. Her first thought to me caused me to laugh: 'Pretty impressive, ah? No hands!' I felt good, very good.

We communicated for around twenty minutes. I asked her some questions and she answered them. We talked about our birth and what she recalled, which is far more than I did! She then hit me with one sentence. I thought I was going to be sick, it left me gasping for air. 'Michael, it was your umbilical cord that choked me.' I got up and walked. I walked for an hour, can't say where, but I got back to the car, eventually. I was shell-shocked.

For two days I was flat. When Pat asked me what was wrong, I just mumbled, 'Nothing.' Can you imagine trying to explain what I had just discovered? The answer is likely, no, no one could. It was three days later when I felt ready for another talk. This time I got up early, at 6am on a Saturday morning, and I was standing with the

Mediterranean Sea up to my knees, the sea relaxing me. Mary made her presence felt but she was sad, the warm glow was not there, it was a dull, cold feeling instead. She communicated that she was sorry, she didn't want to hurt me, and she thought I knew all about her cause of death. Nothing came into my head, it was blank. I felt she was crying, but I can't describe it. She communicated she didn't want to lose me, I was her only contact, our older sister won't communicate with her. She repeated she didn't want to lose me.

I sat down on the beach, and in a long-drawn-out conversation I asked her to join me as I walked up to the Villa de Los Espiritus, as I believe my older sister had made her presence felt there six years previously. I had also encountered a young child there that I could not explain – this I describe at length in the first book of the trilogy to come. As I got to the lane that the Villa de Los Espiritus fronted on to, the hairs on the back of my neck stood on end, Mary went cold inside me. I got closer to the villa, Mary's thoughts screamed at me, it was painful and straight into my head. This time it was Mary's turn to finish the conversation, her presence was no longer with me. I walked back to our villa the long way, around the marina. Trying to collate everything that had just happened.

At the villa I wrote in my diary the following statement. I just tried to read it now, it made sense at the time, but maybe not now in hindsight.

'We have never rented Villa de Los Espiritus since that first day when my older sister's presence was with us. No one has rented Villa de Los Espiritus since that day. It is no longer a rental villa at all.'

I finished this statement with crosses shaped in the form of a knife. I believe I was trying to depict death.

The Villa de Los Espiritus has now been knocked down and only the rubble remains.

Just a moment to reflect – September 2019

I cannot say that I am enthralled with writing this abbreviated version of events. I do not feel comfortable with not offering or trying to explain certain situations that have occurred. However, in this new world of immediate information, I can see why my advisers have suggested this format.

I feel quite sad when I see people talking to each other, but having their mobile phone in one hand, readily available to download relevant information to the conversation. 'Relevant' is the key word in that sentence.

Then you get that one moment when the conversation hits the all-time high: 'I've got a photo of that on my phone, hold on a second.' Now, that second, it is allowed to drag on for ten seconds, and after that all interest is lost both with the photo and the conversation. The common statement then follows: 'It's here somewhere. I'll email it to you.' Wonderful, never to be revisited again.

Call me an old cynic, but the mobile phone is now just an appendage of our body, an extension of our brain.

I digress, I have written this abbreviated version to allow people to read this far and decide if they really want to continue or put it in the bin. There are full complete versions being researched and written, with the aim of being published. If that appeals to you, then you may have to wait a little while.

To summarise, I killed my twin sister or should I say during childbirth my umbilical cord killed my twin sister.

My sister is scared of things unknown, she shows fear. Is it the awareness of my negative older sister's presence? I have no answers, but I think I have gained some insight into my older sister, emotionally that is. How I gain insight or contact with my older sister will not be easy, first I have to understand my twin sister's world.

The research relating to my older sister has taken us to many locations: Rudry and Cardiff in South Wales, Cornwall and Mallorca.

I hope by the publication of the next book I will have further information on my older sister.

An introduction into my life from the psychic and hypnotherapist

There are some ground rules that I must first explain with regards to this foray into this mystical world. The first thing I found is that the world was not mystical in any way. It is a commercial business like any other, but people are benefitting financially from a gift that they have developed. We all follow this and live by the same ground rules of life: we have to make money to survive.

The two people I eventually picked to help me in my task were paranoid about their security and rightly so. Would you invite perfect strangers into your house that you have only spoken to over the phone and then discuss this unique phenomenon? I was lead on an intricate trail by both these people. To add to their security worries, they were both women. It took me a full month to find both of these people, to establish contact with them and for all parties to feel comfortable enough to meet. We were going to meet separately, not as a group, my second appointment was with the psychic and three days before that with the hypnotherapist.

The psychic, her name was Naomi, was a communicator with channels not known or identified yet to man, although she did point out that eminent scientists were aware of these channels. When we met, her confidence and style were breathtaking, nothing like I imagined. Her business acumen was the dominant force. She told me exactly what it would cost, no discussion, no negotiations, this was her fee and it was time-related – very precisely time-related – twenty-minute slots, and there would be four of them. Again, no negotiations, after the four slots were completed her communication-management role was finished and I would have time to relax on my own and when I felt ready I could leave. She had made a reservation with a hotel nearby if I needed to rest after the session. She informed me that her clients usually feel incredible strength and a natural buzz when the meeting with the channel communicator is over. This lasts for about an hour and then the client usually feels drained, hence the availability of the hotel, but she did point out that this was at my expense. Nice touch.

The session went really well. It's strange, but I achieved far more than I ever thought I would. I had communicated with my twin sister; she was called Mary. We had established a very slow and methodical way of communicating through thought. It was a communication channel, albeit one that I have never experienced before.

My twin sister was real. What a statement: Mary existed. She was my sister, my dead sister. Our love for each other was apparent; we were siblings.

This was the buzz that the communicator talked about: the high, the adrenaline pumping, the sensation of communicating with my twin sister, who was dead. I wanted to tell the world, I needed to tell someone. The communicator had finished her role, she was no longer my point of contact. I went to the allocated hotel, where my exhaustion brought on sleep, not for long but enough to help me get home. I wanted to tell the world.

The hypnotherapist

Katrina was the hypnotherapist: she was about fifty, well presented and articulate. Her house, well… that is open to debate – where we met was not glamorous nor a hovel. It was functional and comfortable.

Let's not forget this was my first experience of the afterlife and what would lie ahead. Katrina was paranoid about security, and understandably so since she knew nothing about me except from a few telephone calls. Had she done any due diligence on me? I don't know, was it a mistake giving her my real name or did this create a comfort zone for her? I couldn't gauge that, but here I was in a house alone with this attractive female talking about a subject that is not a day-to-day event. The paranormal, the supernatural, the spirit world.

The exact descriptive name and nature of this conversation still eludes me. I was relieved to see that dark lights and a Ouija board were not going to play a part in this session. I had visions of the Del Boy séance in *Only Fools and Horses*, which would have curtailed any meeting, probably reducing it to hysterics.

I wasn't sure what I was going to gain from the meeting, but I had identified, on her instruction, a time and event that I thought held the key to my childhood memories. The event happened when I was approximately seven years old. We had a year for her to go back to. It happened in my mum and dad's flat, so we also had a location. The event lasted four months and involved my mother. I needed to know why she was locked in her bedroom for four months, why I was not allowed to see her. Why did my dad put a lock on the door so high up that I couldn't reach it? So many whys!

The only lead I/we had was from my Auntie Audrey. She told the family that my mum had suffered a trauma and that no one should go to see her. A trauma? Was this a nervous breakdown? What did it mean? For me, it meant that my Nan in Velindre Road looked after me along with the family in the upstairs flat – the Hutchins, they were German, I think their daughter Karen was my first girlfriend. Not relevant at this moment, but it will develop into something that I consider important.

The meeting with the hypnotherapist never reached the end goal, there were too many blockages along the way. There were no drugs/ medication involved, just pure relaxation and some pertinent questions that had me singing so fast that it was impossible to document everything I was experiencing and divulging. It mainly revolved around my father and his girlfriend, Denise. The detail in which I remembered so much about this portion of my life was amazing, if not shocking.

During the writing of this book and follow-up books, I give my father some bad press about this period in the development of my life. I accepted it, I handled it. Please remember how different things were then: we had nowhere to eat together as a family. My mum and dad were working at every opportunity to make enough money to survive. Each and every day of their lives was the same: basic. They were proud, they would not accept handouts, they were survivors.

My dad did not believe in debt and would not buy his council house off the County Council until the very final moment when he was really railroaded into it. He then had a debt of £8,000, not a position he was happy with. His brothers thought he was mad and maybe he was, but my mum and dad had both educated me and they clothed me. They had ensured that I didn't go short of things, no luxuries but we were not desolate.

To try and state what I achieved from my time with the hypnotherapist will come across cold and hard. For my remaining family that knew my dad they may be shocked. Please do not feel less of him. He was a good man – no, he was a great man.

Denise, my dad's girlfriend, was the main point of this session with the hypnotherapist, the role she played in my life and how she engrossed herself with the family. Why I hadn't recognised this before I don't know. The other main point was my mother – was she locked in her bedroom for four maybe even six months because of a trauma? A thought that has always stayed with me was, where did she go to the toilet? Was she really there? I still don't know. I offer some solutions and possibilities in the books that will follow about my experiences with my sisters. We are so close but so far. I am sure as the books develop that bond will grow stronger.

Another setback

Just prior to my proposed meetings with the communicator and the hypnotherapist, I had a call from my researcher, David. He was rather excited and wanted to tell me about a blood line he was following and how it could be the answer to so many questions. He was sure he was on the right track and wanted my permission to spend approximately one hundred and twenty pounds to proceed with this investigation lead. I had no hesitation in saying yes. I had not heard him so animated on the phone like that in the twelve months I had been dealing with him. I was excited, but after two weeks of no communication I was at the very end of the excitement channel and close to despondent.

He didn't like me phoning him. It would cost me, and he didn't like that, his charges included all calls, but I had to do it. No one answered the first call, so I tried again the next day and a woman answered. When I told her who I was I am sure I heard a sniffle, maybe more. I trod carefully and she managed to tell me that David had died suddenly, my file was on his desk, the only file. I knew that he only handled one case at a time. She was crying by now, and it is pretty awkward when you are over a hundred miles away. It was a short conversation and the police were treating the death as suspicious. She didn't want to talk about it anymore. I was useless, offering my help, but in reality I had none to offer.

I have phoned once since, no answer. At this moment the next call is parked as I am awaiting some guidance from above to help me. 'The death is being treated as suspicious.' What does that mean? It is now four months later, and I have heard nothing more.

The psychic, or communicator as she preferred to be called

I had already met the hypnotherapist, and what I found out had no reflection on this meeting with the communicator. She was obviously concerned about security – her security. She had me driving around Hampshire for about an hour. I was jumping through more hoops than a showbiz dog in the circus. I eventually came to a country cottage with a glass monstrosity of an orangery behind it.

We met, shook hands, there was an uncomfortable electricity surge, she went to hold me tight. The shock was intense, and I would have jumped back but she had me in a vice-like hug. It was actually hurting my shoulders and back, my entire body was shaking.

Her eyes were piercing, and I couldn't hold her stare. She led me by the hand into a very open, airy and modern room. I immediately noticed there were no ornaments anywhere, no pictures, nothing to put her mark on the room. She was talking at me, nothing was going in, I looked down at the floor as she led me further into the room. We stopped, she undid my shirt, and her hands went over my chest. I felt a burning sensation, not nice, uncomfortable. Her hands went to my head and massaged it, they felt my scars, especially the long one. The result of an unexplained incident that research seems to indicate may have been caused by the presence of my older sister. She then said, 'These are life-determining scars. You survived.' She pulled my head so that our faces were touching and then pressed, with some force, her tongue into my mouth. I would say for fifteen seconds she explored the inside of my mouth with her tongue, it was painful.

A siren started, a loud blast, two seconds, another loud blast, five seconds, again it sounded. Eight seconds, again, twelve seconds a high-pitched shrill. It then all stopped. I didn't understand but I was focused, my head was clear.

'Lie down on the couch. Your sister will come to you when you are relaxed. I will be back in twenty minutes.'

I lay there, probably exhausted and certainly confused. What the hell just happened? My tongue went around the inside of my mouth, and it felt burnt and sore. With my arms folded I just lay there. Nothing was happening. I tried to think about my sister, what was she like, was she near me?

It then oozed through me: energy, pure energy entering my body. It started slowly, I felt it building, gaining momentum and then it hit me, a jolt which I can only relate to the same feeling as when you are bent over and someone kicks you up the bum... It comes as a shock and a pain and this was exactly the same. Then a large jolt, so much so that I shouted and shuddered. I definitely moved on the bed because of it. Mary and I were one, our bodies entwined, maybe not physically but emotionally and certainly spiritually.

My eyes cleared and I could see the communicator opposite me. I felt good. I stood up, she shouted at me, 'Sit down. We need to talk.' I did what she said, no words, I just sat there. I had another sensation but it was confined to my head, as if I was being massaged, especially my large scar but the smaller scars were getting a different sensation, a softer, kinder massage, but she had done this minutes before.

She spoke slowly but sternly: 'Michael, you have established a communication channel with your twin sister. It is very strong. She has a lot to communicate. I will leave you for another twenty minutes and then return. Do not think of me or your surroundings, concentrate on your sister. She will enlighten you to a huge amount of information about your life. It will take time, be patient. Communication will be hard at first, your thoughts must be precise and your questions short to start with. Don't overburden everything into your first message.' Then the jaw dropper: 'She will tell you about and maybe introduce you to your older sister.'

She then left the room.

Am I dreaming all of this?

I was alone, or was I? I knew for the first time since I started this quest I was scared. Scared of what, I don't know, I was just scared. I needed to clear my head, but that was impossible, questions were hitting my brain at such a rate of knots; I did feel as if I was going to be sick. Then doubt kicked in. 'Michael, walk away. Just walk away.'

Then this came into my head and changed my whole thought process. 'You walk away now and you will never know the truth. I will haunt you for the rest of your life, our older sister will again try and kill you. Don't walk out of my life, you have only just recognised that I exist.' This wasn't my thought process; this was my sister Mary communicating with me. I remember thinking was she threatening me? Am I going mad again?

My mind cleared, my body started tingling, shaking. This was a new experience, and it was pleasant. I felt the tension, the sick feeling and the headache leave my body. I was at peace. Then she spoke: 'Michael, use your mind, talk to me, don't be scared, I have missed you all your life. We are now together, brother and sister.' It wasn't a thought; it was a scream that reverberated around my body. SHIT, was I dead as well?

Our first communication together.
A moment of enjoyment in all this madness

I suppose writing this it now sounds simple: Mary said 'talk with your mind.' It took me a good five minutes to compile my earth-shattering, question of thought to her. Five minutes and this was what I came up with on this incredible moment.

'Hi, how are you?' That was it – bloody ridiculous. I felt her laugh, not through speech but the tingling in my body and the slightest dig in my stomach wall, I think. Her reply showed what I had missed for all our joint lives together but so far apart.

'That's your best shot after sixty years? I'm really well, thank you. I'm dead but having the time of my life. Oh, sorry, I don't have a life.' No tingling in my body, no little jab into my stomach. I felt stupid – I was being told off by my dead sister. It was then that the tingle through my body gave her away: she was happy, we were friends, we were together, my sister and I.

The sole purpose of this book – 2020

I have been asked so many times over the last four years about the presence of my twin sister. This had been instigated by my first book, *Hallucinations or Reality*, and the part that Mary had played in my life. The details of which are thoroughly described in the books that will follow.

There is so much to relate and to put down on paper, it is really endless. Research throws up so many other points that I continue to explore. It was 8 September 2019 that a possible answer was put forward about one situation that had occurred just after the Second World War. It has always puzzled me how my dad came out of the navy and eighteen months later he was in the army in India. From what has been established, the army were short of men. So many were killed or maimed in the War, so many not in a mentally capable state to commit to another military mission. So there originated a type of mercenary army, who would be paid well to represent their country in this new uprising in India brought about by the fight for power over the Suez Canal. It was a cross between the TA and Dad's Army but combat experience was essential. Some would say they were cannon fodder, but in reality there were very few jobs in the UK, no money to spare but families to raise. My father was one of these mercenaries.

This does raise a question about the age of my older sister. Was my father in India when she was conceived? This new-found information will be difficult for me to absorb, but it will have to be followed up to give me satisfaction that I have explored every minute detail of my older sister's life.

My ongoing relationship with Mary has produced so much information to take on board that my quest to find my older sister was still in its infancy. I needed to concentrate all my thoughts on what was happening around me.

The main reason for producing this initial introduction book was to give me some guidance on what I have achieved and where I am heading. It also helps my friends to understand why I am so passionate about any information which might help me to try and understand my life to date. I sincerely thank everyone who has helped me and only yesterday, as I write this, a very close friend brought me some information that in some way confirms a very small point of the energy form that is my sister Mary. This friend asked to remain anonymous.

My aim now is to finish this initial introduction book to my experiences during the covid lockdown period. If I miss that deadline I apologise in advance but it will mean that either I have progressed far further with research than I imagined or, worst-case scenario, I have joined my sister Mary.

I hope it is the former.

Psalm 23:4

Even though I walk through the valley of the shadow of death I will fear no evil. For you are with me, your rod and your staff, they comfort me.

I am not religious, but I feel that this scripture does say something that perhaps we have ignored over the centuries.

Was the presence of the afterlife recognised at a far earlier stage than we can comprehend?

Hallucinations or reality, reality or hallucinations

Since 2015 I have spent a considerable amount of time thinking about what happened during the post operation stages of my incident in Mallorca. There were a lot of things that troubled me and caused me many sleepless nights. The one thing I still find hard to come to terms with was the way medical consultants considered me insane and were prepared to section me. This would have involved me being locked in an isolated room on my own with no communication with the outside world.

The diagnosis of this insane mental state was based on ten questions. Ten questions that classed me as insane because I could not answer them correctly.

I still question whether anyone could answer the questions correctly after being confined in an intensive care unit in Mallorca, then flown back by private jet and isolated in a similar ward in the Royal Berkshire Hospital. During that six-week period I was on copious amounts of drugs. The exact names and dosages have never been revealed to me.

The questions that qualified me to join the ranks of the insane were as follows:

Name – Passed
Date of Birth – Passed
Day of Week – Failed first time, then rethought the answer and passed
Date – Failed
When did the Second World War end – Failed

Who was the last king – Failed

Name the Queen's son – Failed, I said William, stupid but an easy mistake!

What county is Sandringham in – Failed in confusion, Berkshire, no Buckinghamshire, no Berkshire, damn, is it Hertfordshire?

When was the M4 finished – Failed

What sea separates England and Europe – Failed

'Sorry, Mr Richards, you have failed quite a few, we will have to try again next week.'

'Thank you. Could I just point out that I doubt many people could answer those questions after being isolated from the outside world for six weeks.'

'I'm sorry, Mr Richards, they are the questions given to us and set as a standard.' I did ask by who, but it was of no use as I had never heard of them and had no idea what or who they were, although the words 'Cognitive Therapy' were mentioned once or twice. 'Goodbye, Mr Richards.'

That was it. I was just left to contemplate what had just happened, was I insane or just bloody stupid? Five minutes on Google and I would have been walking free.

That period on my own before Pat came in was the longest, most depressing couple of hours of the whole rehabilitation process. No TV to watch, no paper, no concentration. Then the dark side of my brain kicked in: do I want to continue with this whole thing? How could I end it? How many drugs can I get down my throat? What were the best ones to go for? I obviously overlooked the fact that I was still restricted to the bed or perhaps that gave me some comfort knowing that I couldn't really do anything.

Pat arrived and her smiley face brought some cheer to the room but I was not a great person to be with that day. I don't remember contributing anything to our conversation, and I imagine she was relieved to get through the visiting hour and escape to freedom. Can't really blame her.

Sleep would have been a luxury gladly accepted that night but it never arrived.

Hallucinations or maybe reality

Seven days of me devouring all the newspapers, books and TV news that I could. I was going to be ready for the next insanity test. I knew all the answers to the previous test, I was quite confident, maybe even cocky.

I sailed through the dross questions like name, D.O.B, day of the week. I was on a roll. Then it went downhill. What season of the year were we in? What was the Queen's first grandson called? When did the Suez Canal incident happen?

A couple more questions I can't remember and I failed again, with flying colours. Short, sharp goodbye and she was gone.

Looking back on this period, I have to feel sorry for Pat. What a pain in the arse I must have been, no conversation, no glimmer of light in my morose state. A week with her head in a gas oven must have looked attractive at this stage.

Then a bit of a shock. I was told that I was going to be interviewed by a new Cognitive Therapy consultant. She wanted to see how I was feeling and what our next step forward was going to be. I felt quite upbeat, someone was actually going to talk to me about my situation, my feelings, a way forward. Was this my dream ticket out of this place?

When Pat arrived I was quite excited, I may have even shocked her that I had some enthusiasm for life. I told her all about the planned visit. I could sense she was trying to reign me in a bit but I ignored that, this for me was a step forward.

The next day arrived. Again no sleep but that was becoming the norm, I didn't need it. A very smart young lady arrived, curtains were drawn around the bed and we exchanged pleasantries. It was quite relaxed, she asked questions, nothing I couldn't handle. I was starting to feel a bit confident, I could hold a conversation and tie a couple of sentences together. She then blindsided me, ever so slightly and so pleasantly done: 'Michael, there is a bit of confusion as to where the plane landed when they flew you back from Mallorca. You say Aldershot, is that right?

'No, it was Blackbushe.'

'You said it was late and they were going to close the runway.'

'Yes, that's correct, the pilot was running out of flying hours and he did not want to park up overnight.'

'I see, Michael, now was this at Aldershot or Farnborough?'

'I told you, Blackbushe.'

'Thank you, Michael, that is all.'

What I could not understand was that she was not talking about the fact that I had just been flown in on a private jet, with four doctors and support staff and most importantly that I was drugged up to ensure a safe journey. The main point was that I was correct: we flew into Blackbushe!

'Hold on, I want to tell you about my idea. I think it will help my rehabilitation.'

'Well, I don't really have time, Michael, but please proceed quickly.'

I told her that if she sent me home and gave me the same drugs that I was taking in hospital Pat would look after me. A bit of TV and TLC, I was sure, would have me back on my feet in no time...

'Good idea, Michael, I will tell my manager and see what she has to say on the matter.' Off she went. I should have realised, she never took any notes, but I was caught up in the euphoria of the moment. I had a solution and she didn't say no.

Reality

The next day, her senior manager arrived. She looked like a member of parliament. Diplomat's briefcase and a black pencil skirt, matching short jacket and, I think, a moustache or at least the stubble from one.

'Michael, my name is [*I forget*]. I am concerned that you believe your jet landed in Aldershot.'

'I didn't say that, I said Blackbushe.'

'Michael, it clearly states on your admission form that you landed at Aldershot.'

'What? Am I being judged on what I said on arrival here at the hospital? I had been flying for two hours, I had at least four doctors pumping drugs into me, plus support staff and your big problem is that I stated we landed at Aldershot?' I swore too, which didn't help.

'Michael, I will leave now unless you calm down.' Unfortunately, I didn't. I then went on about my idea, the nurse had not even told this monosyllabic Hitler. I was gutted, my escape to freedom had gone and before I knew it so had Hitler.

Pat told me later about them wanting to section me, isolated room, etc., etc. I was now officially insane, mad, up with the fairies, whatever you want to call it. This was my deepest, blackest moment, road to recovery did not feature in my head, death as quick and as easy as possible was my main thought. I sincerely believe I had given in. I was lost in a sea of disbelief. I didn't care. I did not bloody care.

More reality...

I fast forward; a lot of what happened in between has already been documented in *Hallucinations or Reality*.

The year was now 2019, February, back in Mallorca. Second day in the villa and the sun was shining so I went for a walk, nothing too strenuous just around Cala D'Or centre. I wandered back down towards our place but decided to walk down the road behind the villa, passing the scrubland, where most of my exterior hallucinations had happened. It was my morbid interest showing through, I wanted to go back and just have a mooch around. I was not insane anymore, I was back to my writing. Books were flowing well from my brain to my pen, I was in a good place.

The scrubland area behind our villa was dominated by this huge prickly pear bush. It was massive – fourteen-foot tall and probably the same width. In full bloom with dark pink prickly pears it was a beautiful sight. I stopped directly in front of it and could just about see the top. In front of it, closing off the whole scrubland area were boulders, sea wall defence boulders, probably about a hundred tonne of them. It was massive. I couldn't get anywhere near the land. At that moment my mind was racing everywhere, what, why, who?

I remember just standing there staring, not moving. My brain was not functioning, I could not work this out, this couldn't be right. The bank was steep, about three feet down I sat on my bum and lowered my legs. I stood on solid ground, leant forward and pushed the boulder, it was solid, they were all solid. I clambered back up to the path and just sat there. What the fuck was this all about? I remember feeling sick, the bile hit my mouth and I choked and coughed up a good mouthful of the stuff. I stood up and choked again, just bile but the retching hurt. I walked away not really knowing what to do. I couldn't go back to Pat before I could put this into its correct place in my mind.

Little did I know then, how this retching and bile would have such a big impact on my life during the year ahead.

One foot in front of the other, I was in a daze, I kept going. I ended up at the supermarket and thought I would have a coffee. Then it hit me; what about the secret farm? It was only half a mile away. I walked it slowly, worried I would find something, but what? I truly didn't know, but I was scared. I crossed the road and went down the lane. It was strange, the whole of the hand-built wall now had a fence about ten feet behind it, stopping anyone getting in there. The entire site was protected by this fence. It had been made secure, no sign of the peacocks, just a couple of chickens, nothing else.

I walked back home and went inside. Pat asked me where I had been and I said I'd walked longer than I should have and told her I needed a lie down. I stayed in bed all night, just thinking.

Further reality...

Further reality, of what? Insanity or drug intoxication?

Our first trip back to Porto Cristo, the walk down to the church, the blue corridor I travelled through, the corridor of death. I had this vision in my head that this corridor was in the hospital, maybe leading out of the operating theatre, or even the ward. When we went back to the hospital, Pat was treated like a queen on her return. She had gone through a lot of emotions and made a lot of sympathetic friends on the way. It offered me the opportunity to try and clear the blue corridor from my memory or even confirm its existence.

I looked at every wall, every door, and there were little bits of blue here and there but nothing that could give the impression of the blue corridor, the tunnel of death that I remember. I suppose I was disappointed. I asked the basic questions. Had the hospital been redecorated? Were there any other corridors that I could have gone down that were blue? The answers were all negative.

We left the hospital with similar mindsets. Pat was very happy, seeing so many people and reliving that nightmare period now it was over. The main thing was that they were so excited to see us and it was genuine. I must admit I felt the same: they were all very genuine and there was definite joy that I had survived. I forget how many people, men and women, that I either cuddled or kissed. Spanish men don't seem to shave a lot.

We walked from the rear exit of the hospital. I was obviously keen to see the church that I was taken to, where I met Pat's mum and her auntie. Pat led the way because in theory I had not been down that route to the church. We walked towards the centre of the town and I felt this incredible ache in my side. Not like a punch or a kick, but as if something was clamping my gut, tightly. I stopped. I was not doubled up but it hurt as I took a step. I went to a wall and just propped myself against it. The concern in Pat's eyes was obvious. What was happening? Was this going to be a major setback in my recovery? In the place of my near death?

A few minutes passed and the pain eased. I started to look around, and it felt weird. I felt I knew where I was and where we needed to go to find the church. By this time Pat had lost all interest in the church and wanted to go back to the car and get the hell out of Porto Cristo. That was not an option in my eyes. There was an exchange of words and I led the way. I knew where I was going. It was illogical to Pat; I was going the wrong way. She felt that I was leaving the main route to the church. We passed four side roads on our right-hand side. My speed was gathering. I suddenly remembered the crippling pain I'd had, but it was gone now. We reached the fifth road on the right. I looked down it, and at the bottom, half a mile away in a perfectly straight line, was the church. The semicircular tower that I described to Pat was there for us to see. Her logical reasoning that I had never seen the church and she had never seen the semicircular tower were blown out of the water, but, and this is a huge but, the road that lead to the church, a tight, one-vehicle-wide road, was adorned with blue house doors and blue window shutters. It was the most beautiful sea of blue.

There it was, my corridor of death. We walked down it in silence. Pat was, I think, lost for words; I was lost in a myriad of thoughts. It was an awe-inspiring moment. We were at the rear of the church. I followed Pat around to the front and we both stood in front of two massive wooden doors. They dominated the whole front of the church. Pat went to open them and made the sign of the cross. This was not right, I hadn't been through that door, it was just not right. I walked to the left, down the side of the church and there, about halfway down was a single door, wooden but insignificant in comparison to the huge front doors. I stepped forward and opened it, there were three rows of benches, looking directly at a statue of the Virgin Mary.

Three steps forward and I sat down on the right-hand bench. This is where I sat when I had made my last trip to the church down the corridor of death. Alongside me at that time were Pat's mum and her Aunty Kath. They had asked me how Pat was and Kath asked how Jack, her husband, was – he had died ten years before. The bench was uncomfortable, but I sat there taking it all in. It was exactly as I had seen it, nothing was different or out of place. I could not put into words how I felt, I still can't. Euphoria, maybe contentment, it was such a mixture that I felt as if I was floating around the room, just looking and touching everything.

There is no logical explanation for any of this. I cannot imagine there ever will be. You may be lucky and draw a conclusion from these facts, I am not in that position. I still try to analyse it every waking moment, there is no experience that can ever match this. Not in this current life form that I occupy.

Hallucinations or reality? The same question

The incidents that I describe are true facts, they cannot be dismissed with a logical explanation. The logical side of my life ended back in 2015. What has happened since cannot be classed as normal. Certainly not for the average person, and I include myself in this category.

My twin sister has been a great comfort to me and hopefully together we may be able to understand what has happened in our lives. I am in the process of writing the next book, and it goes into events in far greater detail and it is a very fluid account of my life as my knowledge develops.

Some days I think I have made incredible steps forward but they are counterbalanced with the days when I feel that I have taken the same number of steps backwards, if not more. Frustrating is an understatement, but my sister's presence is a gift that I cherish. I hope she feels the same. My older sister: a mystery that one day I hope we will solve.

I made a decision three years ago that I would not touch a drop of alcohol until I either find my older sister or I am satisfied that I have found the complete truth about her existence. I have kept to my word so far although some days when the low ebb sets in it has been difficult, but determination has remained strong.

It is now very much up to you to decide if you want to carry on reading about my experiences and join me on our journey, my sisters and I, or perhaps take the easy step and buy the final book which may possibly be written in three to four years' time.

I do not guarantee a final conclusion in whichever option you choose.

THE CREATION
OF THE AGE OF
UNCERTAINTY

The research and writing of this book has taken four years. It has been both interesting and thought-provoking. I never thought that I would reach this far and still have no conclusion. I would say that I have a rough format of what I have found and how it leads to the conclusion I am going to detail below. I have tried to follow one central thread; the grey areas are within a tangle of the bits hanging off this thread. It is here where I have had to make some assumptions.

You, the reader, may or may not agree with these assumptions. With such a plethora of U-turns in my thought process, you may strongly disagree with what I have written. With this in mind my team have created a forum on my website to collect and collate any input that readers would like to share. We ask that you please be respectful with your comments, and I hope that by creating this forum we, the author and reader, can further educate ourselves in some of the contentious areas of this publication.

The details for the forum are as follows:

www.michaelcrichards.com – mysisterstheforum

Your comments and input will be available for the general public to view. The knowledge we gain from the book and your comments may help to explain life's mysterious tapestry of events.

On a separate page I have listed all the acknowledgements that I wish to make. You will appreciate after four years in preparation there have been numerous people involved in contributing to the notes and research that had to be undertaken to make sure I have been as factually correct as possible. However, I must stress that the assumptions I have made are purely my assumptions, they are based on the information that I have been given but I cannot say they are one hundred per cent correct, that is why I have created the forum, it is for your contribution or interpretations.

There are two areas that I don't think are open to debate, these are the visits/appointments I had with the hypnotherapist and the communicator. These took place as I have described. The contents of the meeting, I would swear on oath are correct. The results I sincerely believe have been reported with sound mind and body, under no sedation or stress.

This point is being handled by Katrina and Naomi with extreme efficiency and professionalism. They were the catalysts to free my mind, and at present I still feel it is work in progress. It should be noted that Katrina and Naomi are not their true names, they both have a strenuous due diligence in place to make sure any clients are not time-wasters and more importantly that they will be safe inviting a complete stranger into their home. Security was paramount in their preparation, and I don't think any of us can argue with that.

The bond that they both created was exceptional, especially with Naomi, the electrical charge between our two bodies could lift you off your feet. I think the fact that she waived her fee shows how productive our meeting was. She learnt a tremendous amount during the time we spent together and it will change some of the directions she was heading in with her research.

I think I must stress here that it is not an easy fix to find out if there is life after death. Katrina was more open about stats than Naomi, she sees about fifty people a year and admits she learns something from each case. However, the majority do not produce the results that the individual was hoping for. She said this is one of the common problems, a lot of people don't know what they are looking for, and they want an easy answer: 'Yes, there is life after death and your mother is enjoying the bingo.' When she explains to the client that they can find out that sort of information by phoning a premium number or visit a circus, the client inevitably gets quite shirty with her. She will now only accept clients that she feels know their ultimate goal not just a glorified end picture.

I hope this has been of benefit to you. It may help you understand how I have come to the conclusions that I have in the following life scenario. There is just one thing I need to add and I know I run the risk of boring you, the reader. These conclusions are mine and mine alone. Patricia, my wife, has helped tremendously with research and has let me plough on with actually putting pen to paper without raising any probing questions. She knew that I had to be one hundred per cent focused in my thoughts and any distraction would have thrown me off the trail I was following.

THE JOURNEY

I think I have established beyond doubt that I had a twin sister. She unfortunately died during the birth procedure. I believe now I know where she is buried and that is within the boundaries of the City of Cardiff, or in those days it was officially in no man's land between Cardiff and Caerphilly. For family safety reasons I will not divulge the address here, but will let certain people know and that I have it recorded. Neither my sister's birth or death was recorded under any authority's records. This may be because of boundary limitations at the time and who was responsible for recording these details. This is still ongoing.

My older sister, well, this was the surprise that ignited the research for this book. Again there are no records to indicate her birth or death. We seem to have established she is five years older than me. Only one person appeared to know anything about her and that was my Auntie Glory, down in Cornwall. Forty-three years ago, Pat had a random conversation with my mum. She told Pat that I'd had an older sister and that she was five years older than me, but it was totally random, and my mother never mentioned it again during her lifetime.

That was the information I started with, but it was the instigating factor that drove me forward in the pursuit of the facts about my older sister. The only one thing I had, which I kept referring to but which also caused me concern, was a photo of a girl in a pram with my mum pushing it and looking radiant in the same year and month that I was born. The photo was definitely not of me. This photo still remains a mystery at the moment. Could this be my older sister? She was certainly a big girl, too big to still be in a pram, but also did not look five years old.

The rest of the information I have been provided with has been through the visits to the hypnotherapist and the communicator. I must not ignore the various incidents that have occurred over the years involving my two sisters. These I know border on the supernatural and cannot be easily accepted.

Before I wrote the conclusion, I decided to seek some medical advice as I needed some logical input. Since my operation in Mallorca, I have been allocated a consultant nurse. We speak every six months to discuss the examination, blood tests and ultrasounds that I have about a month prior to her call. She gives me an overall review, good or bad, but the main thing is we have built up a relationship that encourages us both to be honest with our opinions. She has become a friend, we have never met but we talk about holidays and we actually came across a bit of a coincidence: her name was the same name as the first ship I ever built with Airfix, it was a cruise liner. She has always complimented me on my pronunciation of her name, but at ten years of age it was a big step in my life. That Airfix kit stuck in my mind for many years. The irony of it is that Pat's mum sailed on the same-named ship liner's last ever cruise. Pure coincidence, but a great ice-breaker.

I phoned to tell her that I would be going away and ask if there were any problems with me flying long haul. There was obviously an official answer she had to give but in reality she thought it would be okay. I told her about the preparation of the book and all the events that have happened, especially the supernatural element. She listened intently, I told her everything I could remember and then asked what she thought about a doctor examining me to certify that I am of sound mind and body. She said it could be done, a fee would be charged, it would basi-cally come down to a glorified fit to fly report. If I wanted more then it would have to be a private consultation with a brain specialist, a very hefty fee with the possibility of no results. I said I would probably accept a no results verdict as a plus. She then got very serious. 'Michael, do you honestly believe that what you have experienced is true? You have not embellished it? Would you be happy to take a lie detector? If this goes into the tabloids they would probably want that.'

I thought about it. 'Obviously the last point has to be considered but it will not be my decision alone, it will also have to have the family approval as well.'

'Michael, you have your answer, make sure I am one of the first to get the book!'

THE CONCLUSION

It has taken a long time to reach this stage. I believe I have reached a crossroads with all the facts that I have collected and recorded. I hope it will give me and my family some clarity in this matter.

I have previously mentioned that I have been aware of my twin sister's presence since a very early age. I suppose I never realised until much older how much she was going to impact my life and never in my wildest dreams would I ever have imagined communicating with her.

I don't find it unbelievable anymore and the really strange thing is that I have accepted she is there for me.

I will carry on with delving into my childhood as it holds so many queries that I did not understand or even realise were going on in the early stages of life. It was a simple time, or so I thought. We would get up early, walk to school and then come home and play football. Tea was usually gobbled down as it would be an unnecessary stoppage to our football games.

The main nucleus of the football kids were David Tudge, Gareth Morgan, Mike Williams, Steve Sherlock, Colin Summerfield and myself. We were the bane of some people's lives, playing football on the green area in front of the flats and houses at the end of Heol Penlan. The green was destroyed as a visual amenity, our football used to go into people's front gardens. This would cause tremendous problems to certain older couples in the street who would threaten to stick a knife in the football and sometimes when things got very overheated they would threaten us as well.

David Tudge was our secret weapon – he was small, skinny and, most importantly, very fast. The ball would occasionally go over old Ma Thomas's wall, and we would chuck David in to get it while the rest of us would leg it and hide for five minutes.

Saturday and Sunday were the high-tension days when we used to play football from the time we woke up until bedtime came around. By Sunday my mum would have had at least two verbal sessions with Ma Thomas. These days no doubt people would probably think how cute, they are not strapped to their mobile phones or computer games.

As I say, life was easy, no pressures or stresses – well, maybe Ma Thomas could be included somewhere along the line. So when I first encountered a problem at home, it really went over my head. I remember the night so well, my mother had been in a foul mood all day, doors were being slammed and you could feel the tension in the air. I had been at school all day so I was oblivious to what had taken place before I got home. When we came to sit down for tea, there was absolute silence, no one talking, and I was sat there like a spare part. I even recall what we had: beans on toast. This stuck in my mind because I had given up playing football for this!

My mother then spurted out, 'Michael, you need to know that your father took another woman out for dinner on our wedding anniversary, February the 14th. Valentine's Day!' The rest of this I have already documented and it plays a big part in the trilogy of the books to come, so I am not going through it again. In my little mind it didn't rate as that important, I wanted to play football, to get back outside with the ball. Nothing gets in the way of football.

I realised things had changed after that night, but not really for me. It was only later that things started to gel together and caused me to stop, think and latterly record it.

A summary of how I now see it...

My father had a close relationship with a woman called Denise, who worked with him. In hindsight it must have gone on for years because she appeared in so many situations that even I should have recognised that fact at an earlier age, but it went over my head.

For instance, how did she know the Davises – my best friend's parents? My mother and father did not know them. Why did she end up as our taxi back and forth to the Cash and Carry in Blackweir, for mine and Shane's summer job? Shane Davis was my best friend from school, and he knew about the job as floor assistant before I did. Again, why? My father was the top man at the Cash and Carry, why was I not told about the job before Shane? Was Denise far more involved in all this and in fact had a controlling interest in both my and my father's lives? But why and how did she become that involved? This mystery will unfold I am sure, but at present it still remains firmly in the query file.

Many years later and again a more serious oversight occurred and again in my mind the trail of blame appears to lie with one person. Denise seems to crop up so often in this documented version, I really had no idea of her importance in my life. My big question and one I will never get an answer for, was when Shane committed suicide. Why was I not told? I was not even invited to the funeral and only found out about it three years after when I tried to make contact with him for a get-together. This part of my findings is parked with no further avenues to explore.

There are three other areas of my childhood that have remained a mystery to me and have sat alongside life's other mysteries until recently. That is a long time to have gone unanswered or understood.

There's the tiles falling off the wall in the bathroom, my dad's resulting violence to me, and his missing war medals that were found in a makeshift grave in the garden. I say found, bits of them were. Then, finally, I got the blame for making a hole in the bottom of the fish pond he was building, which obviously let the water out.

Not earth-shattering events but so important to me that they have remained lodged in my brain for fifty years. It was the ferocity with which my father aimed at me, this is something I will always remember and have to live with. Now I look at this and other events and I do wonder, was this my older sister trying to find a way to cause anger between myself and my father. Was she jealous?

I believe I now have an answer and will provide the details as I record the events recently passed with the hypnotherapist and the communicator.

My reason to arrange a meeting with the hypnotherapist was to unlock something that again was buried in the storage bank of my brain. My mother's trauma, why was she locked in her bedroom for three maybe four months? Why was I not allowed to see her? Why was the door locked at the top so I couldn't get in?

I saw the hypnotherapist and I never got anywhere near even exploring this event. It was mostly taken up with the relationship my dad and his work colleague Denise had. I need to make a decision on where to go with this but that will be raised later.

There is another question I want to try and delve into with regards my mother's trauma, was she actually even in the room? That has come about from the complete lack of information I managed to put together from other members of the family. It was all dismissed by the fact that my mother had had a nervous breakdown and could not be disturbed by anyone. An easy statement to make and satisfied most people. So this needs to be added to my list. Was my mother actually in the bedroom all those months?

There was a bit of a hiatus then with news of the death of David, my researcher. His last words to me were telling me that he was extremely close to finding answers to my initial request: was my sister alive?

I must admit this threw me for a bit and I wasn't sure I was going to continue with the task. I hadn't met the man, but I liked his enthusiasm for life and his love of his job. I felt a bit useless really. How do you offer your condolences to his wife when you don't even know the smallest thing about him? It was a strange feeling and a strange time for me.

The meeting with the psychic was coming up and in my mind I had cancelled it twenty times and reconfirmed every time. I think, but I am not one hundred per cent sure, I phoned at least five times to either cancel it or confirm it. When I was making the calls, I didn't know which way I was going to go until the phone rang, I then put it down immediately. The decision was then finally taken away from me, I was on Facebook and I saw something that hit me hard.

One of the lads that I grew up with, David Tudge, my young footballing friend, had died. I wasn't certain, so I phoned Peter Ellison, a very old friend of mine. He hadn't heard anything so he was going to phone Frankie Ball.

Nothing was coming back, not until two days later, but there it was on Facebook. David had died on the Saturday, the service was to be in a Church in Cyprus, where he lived. It hit me so hard. I know that every death hits you hard, but now, at my age this one in particular was a bad one for me.

The long summer days of football and not a care in the world, contented with life, this was probably an understatement. Life had to change, we grew up and now we are at the other end of it.

I knew from the moment I heard the news of his death, I had to complete my quest for my two sisters. David, I thank you.

The phone call to the psychic was made. It wasn't an easy task to stay on the line as the phone rang, but I did and the arrangements were confirmed. I am not going to go through all the arrangements, again this has already been documented and will be further mentioned in the first book of the trilogy.

The outcome was astonishing; I don't think I have described the whole episode to its maximum potential. I even thought about hiring a ghost writer to refine my description of events, but I realised this was not what I wanted. This was personal, it was between my sister and I, and I would say our family.

I don't think they will ever meet her or be aware of her presence, but I cannot categorically say! I do know life is full of unanswered questions, and I have ticked the yes box on a few, but so many boxes remain empty.

I cannot say this was the greatest experience in my life – the birth of our children, healthy and well, must be number one – but this probably rates very highly as the strangest experience of my life. For me it was my twin sister being reborn.

'Together we feel no evil as we embrace the Shadow of Death.'

This initial draft has been completed on the last day of our holiday on Jumby Bay Island. It has to be the most perfect place in the world to sit and contemplate life or in this particular instance, life and death.

The one thing I can safely say, is that I do not fear death, but I'm in no rush to experience it. Mallorca was a close call, but a guardian angel saw me through that episode. That guardian angel was my wife, Pat, and she now has an assistant to help her, my twin sister.

THE FUTURE

Therefore, let's try and put this in some sort of perspective. It is possible to do and I believe it makes sense.

I have met my twin sister, we bonded, we can now communicate with thoughts. I was slow to adapt to this but we got there in the end. She has described her life, an energy ball. She is my guardian angel and a good presence. I have a means of communicating with her, albeit very slowly, but it requires work from my side.

I am positive I have or had an older sister. She may be dead – it seems likely but I sincerely hope not. I hope to be surprised. From all the leads I've had, I believe she finally lived in Mallorca. It would explain a lot and why I and my family have been drawn to Mallorca for so many years. It was my first ever holiday destination and nearly became my last.

My older sister is a bad or negative presence; she is/was jealous of me. This is totally my own thought, but I believe my father and mother gave her away to another family. Was it because they had no money and could not afford to look after her? Was she born unexpectedly? Did my parents get their timing right with the planning of my twin sister and myself? I must stress this is my theory but follow the paper trail and it makes some sense.

My older sister's presence tried to kill me. There is more information on that to follow, but the three incidents have stuck in my mind from a very young age: the tiles in the bathroom, my dad's medals and the fishpond. Was this my older sister's way of splitting me and my father at the same time? Again I must reiterate this is my opinion, no one else's, mine alone.

I may or may not have met my older sister's presence, that is still debatable, so at present it's still purely speculation. Whichever way I look at it, I have experienced what form life after death takes. I don't know if it works for everyone, I might be lucky, some call it unlucky. For me, I have met my sister and we have shared some moments together. I like her, she has a good sense of humour. We are truly as one.

Where do I go from here? I don't know, but I will now talk it through with my family. They will need to know the implications. Do I publish it or not? I don't really care either way. I have documented my life for my children's understanding, they can file it, burn it or agree for me to go ahead and publish it. Pat, of course, has to have a big say in this, she has had to live with my determination and mood swings as I have researched and written this.

There have been many wrong turns and so many dead ends but I think I have some clarity now.

It is now 1 March 2020. I have made no further appointments with either the hypnotherapist or the psychic/communicator. To be fair, she told me from the start we would never meet again, so I knew where I was from the beginning with her.

This really started out with one goal, which was to find out what was meant by *my mother suffered a trauma*, which still goes unanswered.

Life or death – my sisters, creating the age of uncertainty

Life

The definition of life has long been a challenge for scientists and philosophers, with many varied definitions put forward. This is partially because life is a process, not a substance.

This is complicated by a lack of knowledge of the characteristics of living entities that may have developed outside the Earth's atmosphere. Philosophical definitions of life have also been put forward, with similar difficulties on how to distinguish living things from the non-living.

Legal definitions of life have also been described and debated, though these generally focus on the decision to declare a human dead and the legal ramifications of this decision.

Death

Death is the permanent cessation of all biological functions that sustain a living organism. In many cultures and religions, death is more of a process than a single event. It implies a slow shift from one spiritual state to another.

A vital commodity of the life form is 'Adaption Energy'. It is seen as a resource that has a finite supply and is provided to the body at the time of birth.

It has been demonstrated that oscillations of the health of the body take place when the adaptability is almost exhausted.

Adaption energy death occurs when the resource is finally exhausted.

My Sisters

A human dead body must always be reported by law. This is to ensure that it is disposed of correctly and to avoid any diseases that are contained in the decomposing body being passed further into the human food chain.

Neither of my sister's deaths were recorded in any format. They never existed, along with another two million people. That figure is an estimate and from the research I have done, I think it is a very low estimate.

16 December 2019 – did my older sister play a part in this decision?

At Christmas 2018 I told the kids and grandkids we would take them to Disney in Orlando. For myself and Pat this would be the last time that we thought we would have the energy left in our bones to do such a trip. There is so much to see and do that even the fittest members of the family struggle to keep up. The grandkids usually peak about 9pm and are fast asleep wherever they happen to be, sometimes even in their dinner plates.

We were pretty confident this time that we could cope, we would have Justice with us, who being twenty would hopefully be able to manage the exhaustion better than most of us. She had been coming with us since she was four and is our daughter Rhian's goddaughter.

Unfortunately, during 2019 I came down with a very annoying medical condition. I now realise, writing these last chapters this condition took place in Mallorca in February 2019. I have already described the incident that introduced me to this medical problem earlier on in this book. It has resulted in the fact that occasionally I have a gut problem. It's very hard to explain but I am going to try.

It usually starts with the slightest stomach cramps, not direct pain but uneasiness in that region of the body. Within an hour the pain kicks in and I cannot sit down, I cannot stand up. I now usually find a bed and lie there waiting for the inevitable to happen. It seems to be set to an exact time, and after another thirty minutes I start to retch and vomit. When it first started back in February 2019 it was just bile not full-blown vomiting.

Alongside the diary that I have kept relating to my experiences with communicating with my twin sister, I have logged this condition from the start It would occur every four to five weeks; it was short in comparison to now. Initially the attacks lasted for about an hour and then it was as if nothing had happened. Now they can last two hours and leave me totally washed out. I am useless for the day when it takes control of my body and the following day. I have to spend most of the time in bed, not sleeping, just lying on my back.

The period between these events has shortened, from five to four weeks, then it reduced further to about every three weeks and now it is almost every ten days.

Therefore, on 16 December I had to tell the family that realistically I would not be able to make the Florida trip. Many tears and irrational thoughts but I still wanted them to go for the grandkids' enjoyment. The grandkids had been doing tasks all year to earn them spending money for Disney, so they could not be let down at the last moment. That would have hurt me more than anything.

I had a meeting with my consultant on 23 December and they came up with a plan to alleviate my problem and to give me confidence to plan at least a week in advance. It was a small thing to ask for as a Christmas present but it would bring my life back into some normality. The most frustrating thing is that I am checked on a regular basis and yet they cannot find anything that would cause this situation.

I know I am obsessed with my twin sister and my older sister, but my memory goes back to the lifesaving operation in Mallorca. Even though I was totally drugged up on propofol, Michael Jackson's favourite drug to end all parties, I remember very well the nights in intensive care when I had so many drips connected to my body it was like I was wrapped in spaghetti.

Each night I was there on my own, my body was useless but my brain was still working well, one particular drip line would come out of my body. The night staff nurse would scold me on every occasion that it happened and it happened most nights for a week. That's my insane mind calculating that week period by the way. The nurse would rant and rave at me, but I couldn't reply, there were too many tubes going into my mouth. I wanted to point out, how the hell could I pull the bloody tube out when my wrists were strapped to the bed along with my legs. I have no idea what drug the tube was supplying. I only know they were using Michael Jackson's drug because the doctor told Pat. No doubt a great comfort to her at the time!

It was interesting for me that the night staff nurse was not present when we went back to meet all the team at Hospital de Levant. I found this strange as the rest of the team were there including the other members of the night ward team. If only I was of sound mind at the time, I would have tried to work out if the tube was pulled out on the nights she was not there, but unfortunately the drugs played havoc with such precise facts. The one logical thought that remains in my mind was it was my older sister's presence that was removing the tube. I use the word 'logical' slightly tongue in cheek. In the book of life, I am not sure how they detail what steps you should take when your older sister's negative presence tries to kill you.

Where this all leads to I am not yet sure, but the Disney trip, for me, was a huge psychological blow that left me questioning whether to continue with this uncertainty. It was extremely hard to get my brain back on a level where I could feel enthusiastic enough to even get out of bed.

In moments like this you do have to contemplate giving up life altogether, but I was lucky, the feeling came and went.

My twin sister – the family
18 December 2019

Now that I have established contact with my twin sister, I treat it as a normal event. I have stopped apologising for talking about it and no longer feel that I have to explain my sanity. The correct word is comfortable, I am comfortable with this fact. Another strong word: fact. Interpret it as you want, I know what I mean when I say it.

My family sort of accepted the fact, but not with any great enthusiasm. I understand totally why there is a lack of belief from Pat, and that is because of her religious upbringing she cannot understand why her deceased father or mother have not made contact with her. Will she ever believe? I cannot answer that, only time will tell.

Daley, my son-in-law, and Lee, my son, will listen and they don't take the mick, but I'm sure that they think I still believe in Father Christmas.

Rhian, well, I think she wants to believe but family peer pressure is hard to overcome. I do honestly think that at some stage there will be circumstances that cannot be explained and this is what will convince her.

Where I am lucky is no one has ridiculed me and I in turn have not forced it down their throats. So there is a passive equilibrium in place.

My twin sister, Mary, is part of the family as I see it. She has her views, we have not explored these as yet, too many life-changing questions to ask. I know I do bore her sometimes, trying to ask questions that professors far more qualified than me, two in particular at New

York University, have researched for many years. I like to think that I am closer to answering those questions through my twin sister than they are with their research. When and if I share this knowledge with them is undecided. That will have to be my decision alone.

I now have to wait for the meeting with the Gastroenterology consultant. I feel very strange; I do not have any idea what he is going to say or do. The thing in my mind is that I do not really care, I will accept whatever he tells me, I do not have the knowledge to argue or the will to prolong any conversation. I need something done to start living a normal life.

The decision not to go to Disney was taken out of my hands when the consultant told me I was not fit to fly. It was the right call and I will be happy knowing that the kids and their kids will be enjoying themselves. It will help ease the discomfort of the operating table when it is eventually decided what they are going to do with me.

I am going to carry on with the books and communication with my twin sister, exploring every possible avenue to find out what happened to my older sister's life. I have come to terms with the fact that it is very unlikely that I will ever find her alive.

I await the consultant's examination and see what joys that holds. So many things are happening that it is impossible to draw a straight line across the resulting events.

The publication of *My Two Sisters* will no doubt provide more questions than answers, I feel that I have only skimmed the surface with this initial publication, and there is still a very big ocean of life and death to explore.

My aim was to introduce the experiences that have occurred since my near death in Mallorca. I hope my description of events has enlightened you to the possibility of some sort of existence after death.

Enthusiasm low and the blows keep on coming
19 December 2019

Kevin, Pat's cousin, was receiving his MBE at Buckingham Palace. A great honour for the family. We were invited to the celebration in the evening at the Richmond Harbour Hotel. Unfortunately, the day started badly for me because I had to go into the Royal Berkshire Hospital for blood tests. The taxi arrived and I was just about to get into it when the cramp in my gut started playing up. I had to make a decision: do I continue and risk being sick in the car and then suffer vomiting attacks for the next two to three hours? I just couldn't face it, so I gave the driver a tip and told him to cancel the journey. The frustration was immense, this was the second time in a week that this had happened and the attacks were getting more frequent and more potent in their strength.

I went back into the house, swore with frustration, went upstairs with a bucket and waited, sat on the edge of the bed. After about half an hour I relaxed a bit, the cramps were not so intense or building as they usually do in the first hour. I gingerly lay on the bed with the bucket by my side, where I lay all day, falling in and out of sleep. I thought to myself, if nothing happens I am going to Kevin's party in the evening.

Come four o'clock, I decided that although there was a risk, I felt confident I could get through the night without an incident. I showered, shaved and started to get dressed. I was still coughing from the cold or flu that I had but no intense stomach cramps.

I went into the bedroom to show Pat the shirt I was going to wear, it was dark blue and I wanted her approval that it would go with the jacket I was wearing. I had a sudden cough and splutter, and some saliva went onto the shirt. I went to wipe it off with my hand and Pat told me to stop, she would do it with a flannel so it didn't stain. It looked fine as she finished, obviously wet, but okay in my eyes. Two minutes on the radiator and it wouldn't show. Pat went into the bathroom, then I heard her say, quite loud and commanding, 'You had better see this.'

The flannel had blood on it, not just a spot a big stain. No words were spoken, I just went back to the spare room and lay on the bed. I knew that Pat had to go to the party whatever happened, she and Kevin had been like brother and sister since a very young age as they had all lived together in the same house. She could not miss it, and with Daley and Rhian going with her she just had to go. I knew she was scared, so I put on a very false brave face. The taxi picked her up and I was on my own, she would not be back for five hours, and five hours is a long time to contemplate life.

Five hours later
Thursday 19 December 2019

Pat came home and I was downstairs waiting, four of the five hours I lay on the bed. There was no clarity in my thoughts, no space where I could find any logic in my brain. Nothing made sense and my brain was either in fast forward mode or total rewind.

I listened to Pat when she came in and sat down. It was obviously interesting to hear about Danny's (Kevin's best man) speech, Kevin's reply, how all the children had developed into their adult stage of life. She went into great detail about how the taxi driver had got lost going to Rhian's house for the initial pick up. This was real life, something I could grab hold of and relate to, it meant my brain was not at break-neck speed trying to cram all my life's experiences into the five-hour interlude when I was on my own.

I did have a slight smile on my face – there was Pat looking resplend-ent in a royal navy blue lace dress and me in a pair of trackies with my lime-green bucket by my side, a great Instagram moment.

It was about 1am and Pat had to go to bed, she was out on her feet, she also had the flu and was feeling rough. We slept in different bedrooms, my bucket and I were not the best bed mates to have along-side you when you're not feeling good yourself. Sleep did not come easy to me. I read garbage for a couple of hours and decided to get up and do some research on the Suez Canal and why my dad was there. I went back to bed for an hour at 5.30am, an hour was all I needed.

A day of two big decisions
Friday 20 December 2019

I took Pat a cup of tea up to bed at about 8am. We sat and chatted, she telling me all about the previous night. It was mostly the same story as she had already told me but with additional detail. She asked what I was going to do about my blood tests at the hospital. That for me was an easy one: I would phone the nurse who is allocated to my case, Eriana, and see what she had to say. I would leave it till 9am, until she arrived at her desk, and take her advice.

I went back down to my office and continued sifting through the many leads that had been generated from my Christmas message on Facebook and LinkedIn.

My phone rang at 9am, it was Eriana. She had noticed that I did not turn up the previous day for the intended blood tests. I told her the story and she apologised, but what for? I said it was not her fault, the fault lay entirely with my gut. I asked if I should try and return today. She said yes but to leave it for a while as she had just left there and the clinic was rammed, I would be sat there all morning. She would phone me about midday and let me know the situation.

Pat must have heard me on the phone, because as the phone call ended, she entered my office. I went through the conversation exactly. Pat sat down. 'What are you going to do?'

There was only one reply. 'Follow Eriana's advice and wait for her call.'

Then Pat said something, not in a nasty way, no way was it malicious, in some ways totally innocent. It hit me in the gut far harder than any cramps that I had experienced in the whole of the last year. She told me that Rhian had seen my post on Facebook, which gave an update on my book's situation, and that she didn't understand about my lost sister. I asked Pat what her reply was, the reply shocked me, because she did not understand the situation either.

I said that she was there when I told the family about my twin sister and my missing sister. I had explained that if they don't want me to go ahead with it I won't. Everyone agreed for me to continue writing.

The second time I told them, about two months ago in Rhian's kitchen, everyone was happy for me to proceed with research and the book. I had to ask Pat, what more can I do?

Pat replied, but it was then I realised she did not know anything about what I had been doing and what had taken place, nor did the family. In hindsight, I should have recognised this at the time I was telling them, but perhaps I am too involved in my quest to take an overall view. I knew, because of Pat's religious beliefs, she could not accept anything that was not black or white, but I had felt that she understood my situation. I was wrong.

It was probably the first time in my life that I really didn't know what to do, or how to handle it. I made a weak excuse and went for a drive. I went up the lane to Crazies Hill, apt name, and just parked up on a secluded bit of land. It was 9.30am, my Friday had been destroyed, what else was to follow?

I sat in the car for an hour and a half, just watching the wipers brush away the rain, back and forth, back and forth, my brain in freeze mode, my eyes following the wipers.

On the left-hand side of my brain I thought about the definite offer of a film based on my book, maybe even with me in it. I also had interest from one of the main media streaming companies. Six people directly rely on me for their employment.

The right-hand side of my brain would balance the left back out. My family had no enthusiasm for the book or what I was trying to achieve in finding my lost sister and what happened to her and my twin sister's presence.

Back would come the left-hand side, and that side of my brain was becoming overloaded with reasons to continue, but in all reality, the thought that I had probably wasted four years of my life was starting to win the battle and I was starting to accept this more and more on each right-hand swing.

At 11am I had to make a move because I was having a meeting with Asya – she has helped me in the last two years with photo shoots etc. She was not one of the six people I mentioned earlier but she did receive income from me for her work. She wanted to give me a Christmas present to thank me for my help. The decision was made as I drove to Asya's: I was knocking the book on the head. Asya would be the first one to know. I felt sick but somehow relieved. I had made the decision, the book was no longer a problem in my life, now I needed to get my health sorted.

La Fontana
Friday 20 December 2019 at 12.30pm

Myself and Asya had been talking for about an hour. She had given me my Christmas presents and they were gratefully received, especially the print of her mum and me back in September.

I asked how her mum was with the bomb going off in Moscow and the shooting. Asya told me she was far enough away from the event in Moscow not to be in danger. This came as a great relief, but also highlighted my ignorance of any geographical knowledge of Moscow, in fact Russia as a whole. It was good to hear Asya tell me how her mum had told her friends about meeting a famous author in Britain and how much we enjoyed each other's company. I promised next time I would take her to see a local brewery since she once worked in an equivalent one in Russia.

Asya was sending her mum the same print that she had given me and her mum was very excited, again she wanted to show all her friends. It meant a lot to her, and in all honesty, it brought a glow to me as well. Little did Asya or her mum know just how much it meant to me. There was a small doubt rearing up about whether to tell Asya that I was not continuing with the book about my two sisters. That doubt grew considerably when I saw what Asya had put on her Christmas card to myself and Pat: 'Thank you for being such an inspiration for me.' We hugged and left to go our separate ways, my brain again flopping from right to left.

Broad Hinton Estate
Friday 20 December 2019 at 4:30pm

I met Helen, a single mum with two children. Our paths crossed a while ago and I have helped her out in a very small way. She told me she had been without a car for two weeks so moving around the area had been a little tricky. She had just been to pick up her car as I rang the doorbell, so she still had her coat on. I felt awkward that I was imposing on her. She went into the kitchen with her younger son and came out with some presents, her son was carrying a small box with an inscribed fudge cake in it. He read it to me loud and clear, a very poignant moment for me.

Helen gave me another present and I was feeling quite humble that someone would go to all this effort. There is a hope for mankind. Then I remembered she had been without a car for two weeks, making it even more poignant for me. It certainly started a glimmer of light shining in my clouded mind. We talked for about fifteen minutes, nothing major or world-changing, then she asked how the book was going. I avoided eye contact and said fine.

I went home with a warm feeling in my stomach but a lead block stopping my brain swinging.

The inscribed fudge cake has no significance to the story but to me it meant so much. Someone had gone to the effort to organise and personalise this gift for me. It really gave me the impetus to continue not just with the book but with life itself.

It also gave great satisfaction to the grandkids as I walked through the door and they piled into it. Heaven and bliss combined.

Kitchen, Lake Lodge
Friday 20 December 2019 at 5:30pm

The phone rang – it was an old friend from Cardiff, Neil Price. I had spoken to him about including his unusual contribution to this book. I was worried about actually using his name, should it cause him any problems.

It came as a welcome surprise when Neil told me he was comfortable with me using his full name, he didn't need the comfort of a pseudonym. He started to give me the facts of his particular situation and at first I just listened, then I realised that with such a cross-network of family events I should be taking notes.

His surname, Price, has been abbreviated over the years and everyone knows him as Pip or Pippy. This is where he dropped the bombshell: his surname was not Price at all because his grandfather's surname, was not Price. His grandfather's surname was Tippin. His father had been given away for adoption at birth because Mr and Mrs Tippin could not afford to keep their baby. His father took the adopting family name of Price. This was not recorded and forgotten as time went on. This was wartime and drastic decisions like this were commonplace. Money was tight in the South Wales community at the best of times, the War increased the pressure on families and incredible decisions had to be made just to survive.

The surname grew with the child, hence my good friend's surname became Price by default, although if there were accurate records registered it would show Tippin. No one asked questions, everyone knew this was a commonplace event. It was a way for Mr and Mrs Tippin to hopefully ensure that their son had at least a start to life.

My friend Neil found out as he dug around that his grandfather on his mother's side managed to get his grandmother's sister pregnant after a row with Neil's nan. His 'real' grandparents then brought up his auntie's child as their own. I could go on and we will be talking over the Christmas period of events that I know of that took place in my family and that Neil has also experienced. For me this proved that the events that took place in my family are not isolated, records were not kept accurately, they were often ignored for the survival of the family. That was a point that Pat would not accept but I think I can now put my case to her in a way that shows my family were not an isolated case.

My biggest concern all along is a fact that I stumbled on purely by accident. Around 1950 it was common practice to send the corpses of stillborn babies to America for experiments concerning nuclear fallout and how it would affect the human body Take a moment to think about this, no records were kept, no traces were left and our British government were willing participants, so much so that they carried on with similar experiments in the UK up until the 1960s. The sense of relief that I felt was incredible when I found my twin sister's grave. My only fear now is for my older sister, a rough calculation suggests that she could have been born in 1950.

I have two tools to tackle this, hope and information, and combine this with my enthusiasm, I will get there, some day. My aim now is to relay all this information to my family as accurately as I can and ensure they understand it.

After Neil (Pippy) revealed his details, I thought it would be prudent to review the research results that had already been documented by my team of family tracers.

The simple fact, and it was the main heading of the report, was that neither my twin sister or my older sister's births or death had been recorded. This came to me as a shock three years ago, how could this happen, who was deliberately hiding these dates?

Now, on a closer review of my family history these two omissions are quite minuscule in the bigger picture.

My father was one of seven children: Olwyn, Joyce, Betty, Gwyneth, Mansel, Dennis and my father, John. The records indicate that only two were ever recorded – Olwyn and my father. Joyce, Betty, Gwyneth and Mansel never existed. Dennis was the youngest of the family and his presence was recorded at a later date, but not his actual birth.

The history of the family I found quite fascinating but I have made a decision not to go into it in any great detail. There are too many younger additions to the family these days that would not understand the circumstances around how life was an existence back in our parents' and grandparents' days. Many things that happened then would be frowned on now, but it certainly was the survival of the fittest or cleverest that helped us all to establish our own paths of life.

My grandfather was an interesting character, his occupation was a farm bailiff, and my father's birth certificate details his father's occupation as farm bailiff and then in capital letters 'EX ARMY'.

John Charles Richards was my grandfather's name – my father was also called John Charles Richards. My father left the navy and within twelve months was fighting in the dispute over the Suez Canal for the army. When I found out that my grandfather and father had the same name, I thought nice thoughts – how sweet that the name had been handed down – but now I am a bit more cynical. Was this a deliberate plan? Is that how my father swapped from the navy to the army with such ease? Why was my father's birth recorded and none of his brothers? Was there a bigger picture that I should explore, maybe!

My grandfather, the farm bailiff, sounded a right character. His job entailed collecting rent, and getting rid of tenants who failed to pay their rent and who did not produce enough crops for the landowner to sell. He features quite considerably in parish records, not someone you wanted to cross.

I think Pat may have to come to terms that black and white sometimes morphs into grey, especially where government records were involved. The forces records were an even darker shade of grey – amazing how many boys added two or three years on their application into the army, navy or air force. They went from boys to men overnight, on paper anyway. Unfortunately, the most accurate of records still appear to be gravestones, and during the periods we are researching there are far too many.

2020 – The initial introduction to *My Two Sisters* completed

To my family and close friends.

Dear All,

I thought it appropriate to finish this initial publication of *My Two Sisters* at the very start of a new decade.

January, for me, is going to start with a flurry of hospital appointments. I hope by the 10th of the month it will at least be identified what is wrong with my stomach and connecting tubes. All indications suggest that there are some problems with scar tissue which is affecting my digestive system. It seems to make sense to me and I just hope that is all it is.

Not being able to enjoy Christmas dinner was the final kick in the teeth after a year of not feeling confident in arranging any dinner dates, meetings, or even going to the cinema, not knowing if stomach cramps were going to kick in and then result in the vomiting that would follow and last for two to three hours. It has been a pretty frustrating year in fact and one that can disappear from the memory banks as soon as possible.

The research and writing behind this project has kept me going through the dark moments and has at the very least kept me focused, it has ensured my enthusiasm, it drives me forward. There have certainly been many surprises along the way, some believable and others, well, I have given you my interpretation, it's your choice if you believe what I have written or not.

I will repeat again that without the help I have received from everyone I would never have been able to produce this initial book. Something so irrelevant to yourselves, when fitted into the bigger picture, has revealed so much and opened up doors that were originally firmly shut.

Thank you once again for this information and treating my emails, texts and phone calls in the way that you have. For me it has been a big step in not having to apologise before I ask the question, or trying to say in a roundabout way 'I know this sounds crazy but could you' etc. This is a small step but has been very important to me.

What happens now? Well the interest has been incredible. I have one definite offer from a TV and media company that want to produce the books, my story, into a film or series. I have another large player in the industry showing more than just interest, they are pushing hard for me to firm up on my commitments.

Do I really want to go down this road? It is a big decision. It's all very flattering but I have not even started writing any of the main books in the trilogy of *My Two Sisters*. I do not want this to develop into a disrupting factor that makes me take my eye off the ball and deflect from the main reason why I am researching and writing.

That aim is relatively simple: I want to find out what happened to my older sister and how she coped with her life, could she still be alive? Then, the obvious question, where is she?

My twin sister is slightly easier because I now recognise the existence of her energy source and how, roughly, to communicate with her. I need to explore and understand more about her existence and find answers to so many questions I have.

I know none of this will happen overnight but there is some urgency on my part to move things on as quickly as I can.

The tests that I have undertaken in the first ten days of 2020 have proved negative, which is tremendous in the sheer fact that there were no traces of cancer cells or anything untoward. However, it has left me somewhat deflated knowing that I still have a problem that can occur at any time with the stomach cramps and resulting vomiting. The restriction this imposes certainly restricts any commitments I make. I will have to live with this until the consultants decide on what other avenues they should follow.

To finalise this publication into my research on my older sister and the experiences I have had with my twin sister, I feel that I must state once again that everything I have described, hopefully in some under-standable language, is totally accurate and true. I have tried not to embellish it in any way, but please understand that I may waffle on a bit too much. I am not a professor of languages.

Things are progressing at a rapid pace and I will carry on with my diaries, as it is the only way I have to try and reflect on what is happen-ing and how to understand these experiences. Please bear with me.

In our current situation I wish everyone a safe 2020, we all realise that we have never had a year like this and we can only hope that the worst is over. I hope we are able to celebrate Christmas in the manner we all enjoy, but most importantly, stay healthy.

My sincere best wishes,

THE
GENEALOGY
CHART

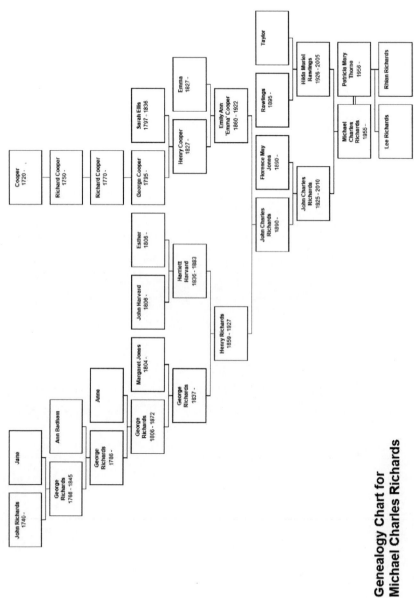

**Genealogy Chart for
Michael Charles Richards**

On the opposite page is the genealogy chart I used as a base to start the trail of my ancestry. It was useful but its accuracy was far from the final solution.

The new genealogy chart is so big and vast that it occupies fifteen pages of historic script. Too unwieldy to publish in one document, the explanation for this is that records were found to be so inaccurate or non-existent that the only reliable form of information was obtained by reverting back to gravestones. Obviously, the war caused so much upheaval that the records, although important, were not kept up to date, understandable in those harsh years of survival.

I will one day publish the full genealogy chart, but it will not be my first priority. It is a working document that needs interpretation every time we consult it.

How will our grandchildren's children view such a document? No doubt by then it will already be included in their metabolic structure.

My Two Sisters
The trilogy

The development and publication of the trilogy of books is work in progress. So much information is being generated by the research team that it is causing me to change my direction of writing in so many ways.

Just when I think that I can finish and close that chapter another small point arises and I have to reshape my thoughts to adapt to this further input of data. The completion of the trilogy of books will very much depend on my experiences and my health – the experiences will continue, it is my health that causes me a larger concern, but with my two guardian angels by my side, Pat and Mary, I am sure our little team will give it their all.

My aim is still to produce at least one book a year. The first publication of the trilogy relating to my complete story is nearly completed, to the first draft stage, that is. This is where the hard work starts, proof-reading, accuracy of research, dates etc. The use of correct grammar and so many other inputs that it leaves me feeling like a scolded kid with so many mistakes made.

Usually by the time the book arrives back on my desk, I don't actually recognise what I had originally written, although I am told that people will find it easier to read and more importantly understand what they are reading.

To keep up to date with developments visit my website:

www.michaelcrichards.com

If you want to purchase *Hallucinations or Reality* that is also available on the website. It was first published in 2016, and a lot of things have happened since then!

POSTSCRIPT

With the trip to Disney cancelled I must admit I was not in the best of moods come January to commence the ten days of tests to try and identify what was causing me such trouble in my gut area. Obviously the big fear was that there were cancer cells present, and then the inevitable months of treatment ahead. It was a long ten days, with visits to four different hospitals in Berkshire. No two hospitals were the same, many positives and similar negatives. If Trip Advisor ever want me to rate each one I certainly have some interesting notes that I scribbled while waiting in between various appointments.

The results of the tests would be ready for 21 January and an appointment with the consultants was made for the day immediately after. The news was good, all the tests were negative for cancer cells. My internal organs were working well and there was no sign of any distress around my gut, except for some bruising where various tubes and needles had left evidence of their presence. Absolutely great news, but it left me with a very important question: what was wrong with me? A question that I felt was quite important, but it was appearing to be overlooked. When the consultant said there would be no need to change the medication as the drugs seemed to be working correctly, I lost my cool a little. I then went into a long explanation of what happens to me – I cannot move, I cannot eat, I vomit for four hours and I am drained for about ten days. I seriously contemplated suicide as the only satisfactory option. I followed up with, 'You think the drugs are working well!!!' I did manage to control any expletives.

The response was deafening, no eye-to-eye contact, a huge amount of paper shuffling and then a noise from the lead consultant. He tried to explain that they had followed all guidelines laid down for my case. They had completed the whole examination process well within the fourteen days required and had confirmed that there is nothing recorded that causes them any concern. I politely explained that it was causing me considerable concern and life threating pain. The conclusion was that I would require further examination and that they would come back to me within a fourteen-day period. I reluctantly agreed and prepared myself for the wait, hoping that I could ride out any other attack. It was seven days later that I received a call from one of the consultants whom I had met a few times and remembered quite well because he was actually Spanish. His introduction was short and sharp, he had come across the much discussed DVD of the operation, something that had gone missing as soon as I arrived back in the UK from Mallorca. He did not go into much detail but hinted that he would like to talk about the operation; more importantly to me, he wanted to talk about the possibility of interference by my older sister in my recovery process whilst in Hospital De Levant in Porto Cristo, and then he added the fact that I was on the drug called Propofol that was actually identified as the main reason behind Michael Jackson's death.

Propofol is a powerful sedative that has extreme effects on the kidney, which usually results in kidney failure. It also assists sepsis in its attack on the body's immune system. He was trying to establish how long I was on this drug, and when in the recovery process it was being used.

I struggled to absorb the facts that he was throwing at me: kidney failure assists sepsis, but these were the two main factors that were killing me. Was I being stupid? I asked him again, and he confirmed what he had said.

Then it hit me like a sledgehammer. When I was still in the intensive care unit at Hospital De Levant I was on various drips, but one that went directly into my side kept coming out during the night when no one was around. The night staff nurse would go crazy with me, she would shout and swear at me because the alarm would go off and call her away from her cosy office to come to my bed and re-insert the tube. She kept accusing me of removing the drip. Despite the fact that I was heavily sedated I could not understand why she would get so angry with me. I was strapped to the bed by my ankles and wrists – the scars still remain – so they were definitely not my imagination. I would watch the drip tube leaving my body, ever so slowly, and there was no way I could prevent its removal in any way. Then the penny dropped.

Was it my older sister trying to help save me from my exposure to Propofol? Had I been totally wrong in my initial thought that she was removing the tube to assist my death?

The proposed future trilogy of *My Two Sisters* suddenly became far more important to me and in particular my sanity.

Printed in Great Britain
by Amazon